THE HILL BENEATH

Collected Poems

Colin Morgan

THE HILL BENEATH

Collected Poems

Copyright © C G Morgan 2017

ISBN 978-0-244-33763-6

C G Morgan has asserted his right under Section 77 of the Copyright, Designs and Patents Act 1988 to be identified as the author of this work.

All rights reserved. No part of this book may be reproduced, stored in a retrieval system, or transmitted in any form, or by any means, electronic, mechanical, photocopying, recording or otherwise without prior written permission from the Copyright owner.

First Edition, October 2017

Printed by Lulu.com

Cover photo: *Great Sankey Sky* by C G Morgan

To: Helen, David, Peter, Joseph and Sarah

Acknowledgements

Thank you to the members of the *Warrington Library Poetry Group* and *Warrington Wire Writers* for all the support and encouragement over the years. Also to the magazines and anthologies in which various of these poems have appeared.

And to the poet P J Kimber for her help and guidance during the preparation of this book.

Contents

11	Hello from 2040
12	Hitler's Daffodils
13	My Coma, My World
14	Discovery of a 1936 Riley in a Suffolk Garden
16	And then No More
18	Carousel
19	The Disappearance of Friends
20	One Afternoon on Salford Quays
21	Focus
22	The Hill Beneath
23	Déjà Vu
24	Mayday in Birchwood
25	The Swing in the Tree
26	Balloon Flight
27	Beginnings
28	Night Journey
30	The Fear of Clowns
31	Shadows
32	The First Madonna and Child (of Six)
34	How are we to remember?
36	Human
37	Losing Touch
38	Unfortunate
39	The Death of Anne Boleyn
40	Nuclear Power
42	Formby Beach
43	Lymm Dam
44	We are the Neolithic

46	The Perfect Crime
47	At the Dentist
48	My Designer Baby
49	The Pacific War 1945
50	Brighton Rock Filmed 2010
51	The Price of Milk
52	First Snow
53	Magic Monkey Food (*or* When the Cat is Fed)
55	YODEL and the Squirrel
56	On Reflection
57	Living in the Styx?
58	A Rail against Sedition
60	Message in a Bottle
61	New Town Anarchist
64	Man Apart
65	Sunshine
66	Cyborg
68	The Legacy of the Snail
69	The Day Before
70	Beloved
72	The Silver Pocket Watch
73	Returning Child
74	Stillborn
75	Cycle Path
76	Gandalf and the Traffic Warden
78	Nanobot Hero Soup
79	Stirrings
80	Where
81	Seventeen

82	No Shirt
83	Anne
84	Talking to Elaine
85	Of that Told by Primo Levi
86	Outside Spacetime
87	Sleeping Child
88	Needs Must
89	Death at My Birth Averted
90	Loose End
91	Sonnet 14
92	I
93	Princess
94	The Sea
96	Woman
97	another day
98	It's Easy
100	Justine
101	She Beyond Memory
102	The Lonesome Log
103	Night Verses
104	Desolation
105	Washing Incompetence is Nothing to Boast About
106	Around and About
108	500 Words on the Inside of a Ping Pong Ball

Hello from 2040

I am the first baby Martian,
My parents as familiar in metal suits as dressing gowns,
My world a hemisphere of tech.

My head is light, my limbs slender – I am their Space Monkey.
I would bound around like a lemur, but there isn't the space.

Oh, and your Earth is a star.
I can find you in the sky – a blue point of light against the cosmic pinpricks.
So many stories I have heard – open air, China, Pitcairn Island, camels, London, dragons.
Oceans, flowers, rain.
And people.

Should you ever fall out among yourselves and stop sending our cargo here
we will watch your silent star in the night,
until our eyes close too.

Hitler's Daffodils

Wonderful proud clusters,
Quiet in green shirts on the bank,
Standing tall to herald the inoffensive Spring,
Your shiny golden best is breathtaking.

Nurtured by the nihilistic darkness,
Bulbous in blunt armoured love,
Life is unfolding in floods of sap,
Soaring to parade.

Such unquestioned lemon brightness,
Unbidden in the wicked wilderness,
And the staring little man passes
Distorted, distracted:

Grotesque reflection
Of horror and light.
You remain oblivious,
Uniformly erect in your single pleasure.

My Coma, My World

The news of my demise is premature, but I cannot refute it.
The machine I occupy knows the date and time, but not I.
The radio may speak, sing and dance, but I pay no heed.

My Facebook page is a lasting memorial I cannot see.
I am still sixteen and unformed, but old as a Pharaoh,
and like them, I lie hidden away for an age.

In this place there is no darkness, but my eyes are closed.
There is a chink in my doom, but no light penetrates.
The game is a plan filled with waiting, hope and stillness.

Those that love me are holding me close, far scattered as they are.
Those I love hover around me, and though I am so heavy in them,
they reside as bubbles that float and bump above my bed.

The clock on the wall, watching, makes no comment.
My months are rolls of the Moon, yet the Earth is still.
Medicine may be my true friend, but not just yet.

Discovery of a 1936 Riley in a Suffolk Garden

'Even now there are places where a thought might grow...'
                                           Derek Mahon

Behind the thickened yew hedge of an abandoned house,
among the skips and the scaffold poles,
a family of voles crowds inside the back seat of a 1936 Riley
Merlin.
Their horsehair nests lie within a metallic world,
warm among the dripping toxins and rust.
Why should they crave more?
The generations weave among the jagged steel,
while far outside, wars roll on and civilisations rise.
Their tiny ways are honed to their dark deprivation,
held safe from the kestrels patrolling the morning sky.

Many are the generations, their small bodies mummify –
their home born of neglect in the Macmillan days,
when the slam of a door spelled the final departure
of the aged motorist and his veil of woodbine smoke.
He passed on that night, leaving all to slumber,
except for the voles biting through the leather, the stuffing
crumbling.
Now woodworm and nettles prevail amid the general
collapse,
as occasional sounds reach the dusky inside from afar –
a tractor's throb in the field nearby, the tripping peel of
wedding bells,
or the double crack of a shotgun in the distant wood.

Even now there are places where we can lose a treasure –
African wells, dried and neglected,
filled with death and dust,
a sharp smell lingering in the air, and wire grass
rustling fluid as fire on the desiccated banks;
in the village clearing, where sand trickles into tins,
a dry wall tumbles with a resigning sigh,
a hyena skull bakes dry in the sun,
a bottle winks half buried in the sand;
– and a dilapidated motor car in Lawshall, Suffolk.

Forty years, undisturbed, without even starlight –
no expectation of the ripping back of the door –
until the sudden crack of timber. Explorers, cameramen,
inhale the quiet remnants of pre-war peace.
With furious scurrying, like bullets through cobwebs
and holes, a culture shatters
in the sudden sunlight of discovery.
Meteoric boots land, dispersing these cloistered lives.
Grown away from the hedgerow, living free from fear of the hawk,
their eyes stare back level and expectant from pockets of gloom.

They would wish, of course, in their tiny hearts,
for us to leave them, to abandon them to their warmth,
to close the door and walk away.
Lost species – stuffed dodo and harpooned whale –
the silent island forests and the empty oceans.
'Leave us be' say their eyes. 'Do not rip out our homes –
we that have lived here so many generations.
This is all we know.
Close back the door on this precious space
and let us prevail in our world of peace.'

And Then No More

It is not that there was a sudden rush of wind,
a change in the breeze,
a breath.
Like a Pharaoh's mouth
the gape was silent,
there was no expectation,
no beckoning;
a black hole
with the desert sand a film on the parched lips.

It is not that there was a light of joy,
a glint of promise,
a spark.
Like a Pharaoh's eyes
the gaze was hollow,
there was nothing to see,
no welcoming;
the sockets shells
beneath a bandage of filth across the brow.

It is not that there was a sea of fragrance,
a waft of sweetness,
a scent.
Like a Pharaoh's skin
the aroma was dust,
there was no tang,
mere dry brittleness;
no taste but a soft bitterness
from the rasping snake's skin shed three millennia ago.

It is not that there was a burst of song or wailing,
a cry in the dark,
a whimper.
Like a Pharaoh's larynx
the cords were petrified,
there was no timbre,
no sound but oppression;
the ear felt no disturbance
from the silence trickling long in the tomb.

But there was an imperative,
a need to provide,
to insist.
Like a Pharaoh's life
great power surged forth,
the piling of stone on stone,
a great monument rising;
much adoration and dreaming
and a deep born incestuous love that lingers still.

Carousel

When you contemplate ending it all – where do you see yourself?
Away on a rock with sea rising and the wind tugging at your clothes, sucking you over that edge?
Or perhaps you are sidling into a mirror lake, cold as fingers, slippery as phlegm, to slide from view – to gasp and heave to naught?
Or looking down the long, so long tracks, to that vanishing point, as a bright one-eyed mutant bears down blaring?
Or quietly in the bathroom, the door locked, the water brimming, the razor kind on the shroud white towel?
Or perhaps in the kitchen, the small bottle hard clicked open, the contents scoffed in fistfuls?
Or – I know – in your garage, with water on the floor and a screwdriver in the plug socket?

When you conjure a scenario to do yourself in – when do you see it?
At a brisk dawn, stretching and yawning to meet you half way?
Or as a lobster broiled in the heat of the sun at the noon of the day?
Or at the night's gate where you fade together into the softest bed of dark?
     Enough.
        Enough.
All is sweetness now I hear your voice again.
Clear, and the lark is rising, the moon held still in her arc in blue.
The children are fed and abroad.
The river is deep but steady.
The fish are hiding.
Bring me a flower from the garden and I shall rest a while.

The Disappearance of Friends

Somewhere, there has been a slipping,
a hidden edge, as time continues.
Streaming life has carried you out of reach,
to a new clawed delta of possibilities,
to change the boundaries of your day.

And left, I am sitting here rolling my life away.
Apart, with the string between us snapped,
not knowing which way to reach out
to find my companion of past mists,
with our shared hopes among the everyday.

Like missing a ship, there is a sudden space.
And somewhere, milling round,
your life flows untangled from mine,
our clasped hands wrenched apart,
the fingers' last light touch recalled just now.

One Afternoon on Salford Quays

There are days when
you just know that the girl
enquiring at the kiosk
will walk away
the other way:
not even the small
buoying pleasure
of perhaps
a passing flicker
of a smile to warm the hour.

Yet the high screen
on the wall flickers fire:
a focus ignored –
but see the magic in the flames:
Paris streets.
Shooting.

Man bites cake –
teeth marks in stickiness:
the grey in the sky rolls
like drums.

The face
of Jodie
Foster on the wall
around the corner
like a Big Brother
clock:
comforting the saved.

Focus

That tune in my head again – "Golliwogs' Cake Walk".
Marching men and machines to the horizon.
Beams of sunlight flicker off the brass.
Dour politicians, inflated by loathing, drink-in their might –
their generous expense.

Shrinking...

Turning down a side street,
where cafés, ranged empty like theatres in mourning, await –
their lone monochrome waiters humming, tapping feet.
Eyes follow me as I am quietly detained.

Collapsing in again...

Looking across my cell: Six feet.
A chink of tortured light arrives from nowhere.
Same year, same concrete.
Same Nile Delta stain weeping down the ghost-graffitied wall.

The Hill Beneath

The journey of life happens on a hill; a sugar loaf mountain.

I am crossing the upper slopes, but well past the summit; it is starting to slope down.

In life, height gives perspective; I can see where I am going, where I have been.

The young follow on behind me, still climbing; looking up.

The old are on the final steep descent; looking out into the blue yonder.

And though each day we appear to reach a generous plateau –

We all know the mountain, and its sugar loaf shape.

Déjà Vu

There in the middle distance, beside the road he stands – my father.
He has not seen me. He looks passive, almost forlorn.
The colours around are dim – the suburban clutter.

As I drive closer, I see that it is not him standing there.
Another man, perhaps a father, is there instead.
I pass by and he disappears from my life.

Then I see my father again, in my mind, standing as before.
Perhaps it was him there, though he's been dead these six years?
For that moment, was he not with me, detached, but in the landscape?

And he resides with me now. The dead live on inside us.
Theirs is the world from the corner of our eye,
the broom cupboard of our mind: Reaching out, reaching in.

Mayday 2012 in Birchwood

Hooves clatter on Glover Road.
A rare morning sound in this fresh millennium,
when all our sons stand tall and proud.

Looking through the trees, I expect to see girls
in hats, smiling astride fat horses.
But no,
in a spinning tunnel of darkening time,
I see a horse-drawn hearse –
Dickensian, black, final.
Inside, translucent as a shell,
a tiny white coffin.

My eyes fall away.

It is Ciaran Geddes,
aged seven.
It is his turn.

The Swing in the Tree

It is winter as I pass the drug dealer's house, the upstairs window open.
A hand reaches down and tears at my guts;
a woman inside is wailing unseen
over and over, the gaps for breath,
leaving silent questions with no answers brimming in my mind.

Later, in the spring, another sound – a sharp baby's cry suckled down to a whimper.
A hand reaches down and lifts my heart from within;
a mother letting herself go to love
again and again,
raising silent gladness and warm comfort in my chest.

Now in the summer a tyre hangs out on the tree for playing.
A mischievous hand reaches down to tickle me inside;
the small cousins grin at the end of a rope,
to and fro, to and fro,
the warmth of the day glows into the evening long.

But now it is autumn, the house is empty, the family broken, gone.
A hand stirs a hollow in my bones;
on the rusting skip lies the white mattress from the cot,
piled high and forlorn,
and a vacant insecurity of loss is all that remains.

The Balloon Flight

Preparations are many: the colours among the grass, the gas.
The breeze is a helping hand from the landscape.
Emboldened, the balloon fills and heaves.

Rising, we are borne over to encompass a new perspective:
Silence and movement intensely resolve in a detailed
revelation of our stature.

The company of friends becomes a delicate matter,
a fragility of sharing.
Breathless, we cling to our minimum horizon not daring to disagree.

Slowly we revolve above towns delicate and empty,
as an evening haze joins us in our lazy ways.

Much later, the time to be grounded grows near,
and a point of fear, as a death, springs up among us.

With a rush of ground falling up into our feet,
we are held, gripped, and tipped back to rights.

The end has come, and as a perpetual life
remains unintelligible to us,
so our excursion is closed.

Beginnings

I find myself longing for the life of Cinderella:
The hours of hard scrubbing, the dusty corners,
The black pots, kettles spitting,
the grey ash in the hearth
                        safe to sleep.
While all around, the house bustles with the haughty and the mighty.

Such sweetness in the grime, like a hive in a midden,
Unkempt but secure – safety for the price of a slap now and then.

And the world turns, ripening from Spring to Summer,
The pumpkin swelling, the mice running,
An oblivious Prince waiting in the wings.

Night Journey

Once upon a long year, until it was begun,
A silence blankly reigned, we were devoid of fun.

And never did we realise that time was slipping by,
As the TV yipped along, sapping all our sighs.

Then out from a corner stepped a mystic beast,
Bowing but not smiling, with an invite to a feast.

Out into the night we flew, with all the lights a blur,
Our eyes held wide with fear, on this beast with golden fur.

To a lazy mirror lake, where we set down on a boat,
With lights and dancing shadows, to spend the night afloat.

The eve was young and pretty, the revels just begun,
When out from the blackness, a violent storm did come.

We tightened down the vessel & cowered 'neath the mast,
Sharing warmth all snuggled up, whilst the night did last.

But come the raging morning, with no escape in sight,
Our mystic beast did rouse us, pressing us to flight.

So buffeted and blasted, we flung into the air,
And driving through the spray, soon landed at its lair.

And there among the foul rocks, we passed some hours in fear,
Whilst the creature twitched and glowered, 'til the storm began to clear.

Hungry as we were, we dared not ask for bread,
And the beast was clearly troubled, as it turned to us & said:

'You have followed me too far, too far to make it home,
'You must become kin with me, and now with me will roam.

'The boat is lost, the lights are gone,
'We are the last, we shall be one.'

Then began our third flight, across the swollen lake,
Where the beast's lonely cries, did a potent mantra make.

Now within this barren range, away from Earth and you,
We see life broad and simple, fresh and full and new.

So any quiet evening, with nothing much to do,
Look sharp, content and occupied, or we'll come and visit you.

The Fear of Clowns

On just waking, he is there,
Ragged and broken,
Flopping in front of the firing squad,
His jacket torn,
The flower on his breast crimson, spreading.

I leap up to run, dragged back by the blanket.
Escaping through the ward door, I glance back.
He does not – cannot – pursue,
But his blind hand gropes towards me,
The flower on his breast crimson, spreading.

Fleeing, I dive to flick on the corridor light.
The yellow flash inflates the modern day.
All that remains is evaporating memory.
He is gone to his grave these seventy years;
The flower on his breast crimson, spreading.

Shadows

Their remains are shadows; Laurel and Hardy,
Marlon Brando, the rest,
like the faintest wisps of smoke from a distant gun.

Today, a sinuous and pained old man is kicking himself in the bathroom,
or scribbling an anguished angle of past glory and confusion,
or, maybe, he lies a tissue-stretched skeleton underground
somewhere forgotten.

The singular moment of memory engaging the fanatic's wildest praise
awakes this very dawn on a computer screen near you,
and they howl again, clueless and odourless, in this
unimagined future for a tiny minute.

And, though somehow visible, their tears are dry.

The First Madonna and Child (of Six)

Resurrected from the frailties of human memory,
I have a tale to tell of creation and destruction to bleed the heart.

Not so long ago in the town of St Helens,
John Varley and Co, a foundry since 1843, worked on:
John Varley, issue of John Varley, at the helm;
Horned rimmed glasses, wet eyes behind;
Smooth cobbles leading to the dark oak office
where he sat, perched like a Dickensian bird.

A job to them,
A commission from Liverpool city came forth,
To cast five off eight-foot high solid Meehanite statues of the Madonna and Child,
Cold in iron,
To keep the iron peace on city corners.

The mould was carved – a monstrous sarcophagus with babe in arms,
Featureless as fearful time.
The sand was prepared, sticky like spiders' eggs.
Dead iron was cooked up to a molten river of internal fire,
ready to pour.

The first of five,
She was to take her shape.
The molten life was released, pouring and filling the cavity.
Then, sudden as instant thunder, the mould burst apart.
The dark men cried out and leapt back, sore afraid.

The heavy metal waves inside bid to escape, but froze in the attempt.
Crust and vacuous crevices formed, shell upon shell,
A bursting of gases and energy brought life to the Madonna and Child.
Cold preserved them, like a cave.

She lay there, gasping, a hollow mimic of her intended self
and cooled.
In her arms, the Babe, a fractured thought in iron,
incompletely cast, but fascinating.

Thus she lay cooling and waited but a few hours for her
inevitable fate:
To be smashed with hammers and returned to the furnace;
to become a solid upstanding figure, as per drawing;
to stand like her sisters near the Mersey in the wind, all
aspirations gone.

And Mr John Varley's foundry?
That darkened place with interludes of hellfire: How did she
fair?
She closed within the month.
The hundred-and-fifty-year foundry dance ceasing.
The living tongues of fire gone forever from that place.

How are We to Remember?

How are we to remember? The silence roars in every space
The cold
The abandoned relics of civilisation passed
The desert where the bloated corn ripened once
The river bed of bones where the spawned shoals wove their dance

How are we to continue? Our actions of our own bidding
The ease
The silence beckons but does not insist
The empty rooms collecting the unheeded light
The darkness of evening spreading into walled in night

How are we to love? The distance has stretched the tendrils
The gaps
The goodbyes at train stations
The visits at the heavy points of the year
The tiny call from dots on the other side of the world

How are we to settle? The need has drained dry
The edge
The home waiting vast
The fridge stocked against an invasion
The beds sleeping undisturbed for a season

How are we to grow old? *Anno domini* is relentless
The clock
The lines creep ever deeper
The children approach their middle years
The body leans a little to the wind and tears

How are we to be remembered? The house that was made home
The days
The smell of bread
The piano and the clock ticking
The summer cat and the winter garden

How the family lives on? In the closeness of years
The blood
The additional loves
The new beginnings and growth
The long-shared kinship of the precessing now

Human

We find we are not what we thought we were;
A small piece of God with airs and graces.
Instead we are windbags of skin and fur,
An electric machine that death debases.
Yet our body's made from the dust of stars,
And our brain is super-complex matter,
Our culture dances between peace and wars,
And we fill Earth with music and chatter.
There is no reason to get in a rage
When as it turns out all this is a hoax,
We are just a projection on a stage,
Packed with instinct, ephemera and jokes:
The Universe does not care what we think,
So we might as well go sing, dance and drink.

Losing Touch

The gravy years are behind us,
and wrinkles fold my paper face,
as another dawn lights our eyes from within like beads.

All the ambitions that wrested us from our bed are gone.
We live separately as the unknown,
and do not think of recompense.

We could be together again,
in the succour of our warmth,
basking in light from lost intentions.
Yet the act of going to catch a train,
or climbing into a car,
is beyond us.

We do not even think to pick up the phone.
I would want to run away whilst waiting for you to answer,
that exact voice from a flattened past,
chiming out the same message.

The flow has gone on too long and deep.
We shall never willingly speak again.

Unfortunate

there are small pools of unfortunate
one is on the stairs
they need visiting
in the forever when

larger clumps abound out of sight
they must be avoided
if they manage to join forces
we will be heavy and down

the even silence is the waiting
a quick look
slipping back
a girding is necessary

we cannot ask

The Death of Anne Boleyn

I've kicked it all into the long dry grass;
her head with open eyes fell dead of light.
My tears flow free at what has come to pass.

I had to act from outrage roused *en masse*;
her lying with that minstrel was a sleight;
I've kicked it all into the long dry grass.

Remembering her eyes that shone like glass;
her soft kiss and her sharp love laden bite;
my tears flow free at what has come to pass.

I was forced by the courtly underclass;
the cupped hand whispers; sniggers out of sight;
I've kicked it all into the long dry grass.

Now sweet Jane Seymour is my comely lass.
Yet while my heart bounds to the coming night
my tears flow free at what has come to pass.

A phantom son invades my prayers at Mass;
my marriage to that witch – it was not right.
I've kicked it all into the long dry grass;
my tears flow free at what has come to pass.

Nuclear Power

Unleashed on Earth by the Manhattan race;
a star light wonder shakes us to the core.
Gravely behold, a breathtaking fireball,
whose shock brings about the end of the War.
The focus becomes the hydrogen bomb
and all of us hold our collective breath;

threatened each day that we'll draw our last breath;
destruction seems driven by the Arms Race.
But then a way's found to harness the bomb;
to construct a box to contain the core.
The focus is now on power, not war;
thick walls of concrete hold in the fireball.

In the reactor the nuclear fireball
delivers power with is atomic breath;
for cooking and light with no thought of war;
gifting easy life to our greedy race;
a bounty from its uranium core;
it is meek and mild – don't mention the bomb.

Until Chernobyl explodes like a bomb,
the power station destroyed by the fireball.
Loss of containment; a breach of the core;
countries breathing its radioactive breath.
We tried to stop it but lost the race;
the devastation resembled a war.

But life goes on, like it did in the War;
designs improve to stop another bomb.
A collective sigh from the human race:
'Perhaps we'll avoid a total fireball,
after all?' Maybe, but don't hold your breath;
the next could be worse than fire in the core.

Vast radiation contained in the core
could kill as many as died in the War;
the killer's invisible as warm breath;
as deadly as a virus or a bomb:
whilst those close by are caught in the fireball,
this silent poison can spread through the race.

There have been many cries of 'Ban the Bomb',
but that war was lost with the first fireball;
whose searing breath forever blasts our race.

Formby Beach

The day presents itself as an open book.
We go down lane and motorway and arrive at trees
and dunes.

The sea, she is there too, so still as to be taken for dead,
until a clammy rippling breath in the afternoon
ruffles her goose feathers
to a rhythmic sighing.

Gone are the great guns of winter, all forgiven and forgotten.
We are allowed to stroll along a boulevard of sand stretching
to Southport
and beyond.

And beyond? The ant-sized joys of Blackpool peep over the
lost horizon like broken teeth,
too far to do more than promise a quick sticky kiss.
Hoping for more?

Lymm Dam, Sunny Afternoon Reflections

That swan, she took off on a flight of fancy, her wings
creasing the air, leather on leather, wheezing and scraping,
her brain directing like a tiny Howard Hughes in his Spruce
Goose,
his mechanical swan wide and white with the wing span of
the Dam.
    Have you seen the sun on the water, teasing?
    The untrue reflections,
    Not fooling but dancing,
    Flashing, searing, careless?

I see your open sketch book, the view you have lined up like
a difficult landing.
    Did you get the swan?
    No, but I heard it.
    Powerful bird.
    Yes, but it is so quiet – No breeze.

So, the swan had to heave herself from the mirror lake. Full
power, no help from the wind.
    Can you draw?
    See.
I see.
    When you draw do you put something from yourself
    into the landscape?
    Perhaps.

    I write; poems. I always end up in the poem, but not
    by name, or face.

    I end up written into my poem like a puppeteer
    who extends down the strings to the very toes of their
    puppet.

    So, I cannot let go, I cannot see my performance,
    even in a mirror lake, even on this unblank page.

We are the Neolithic

Forests are spread to the ends of the earth;
humans survive by hunting and fire;
the needs of life are simple as water.
Needles are fishbone and flint is our iron;
our ways as free as the birds of the air;
scattered and few we strive in the wood.

Then clearing by clearing we burn the wood;
soon wide grasslands are spreading round the Earth.
We move more freely in the space and air;
there's a distant view of smoke from our fire;
yet still we use bones and flint as our iron;
but we cover the lands to the water.

The transformation is crops we water;
living in fields on the edge of a wood;
tending the ground with tools hard as iron;
spreading in numbers across the earth.
We take what we want with violence and fire;
we're superior; our cries fill the air.

Our tribes succeed and soon we are heir
to copious wealth on land and water.
The conquests go on with violence and fire
until the hunters have only the wood.
We the farmers spread our tribes o'er the earth
and now we have the wonder of iron.

So our right is ruled by blades of iron;
our religions and war cries rend the air.
Food is abundant from ploughs in the earth;
Our ships give passage across the water.
And hunters must hide in the darkest wood;
we, the farmers, come with sword and fire.

The cities that rise are bred from fire;
thought and language birth machines of iron;
energy mushrooms from coal and from wood.
Vast tracts of smoke fill the blackened air;
our numbers increase across the water;
until farming people fill up the Earth.

Now fire and smoke restrict all the air;
production of iron pollutes the water;
and all wood is dying on our marbled Earth.

The Perfect Crime

If you are reading this after I strangled my tormentor,
then perhaps I should have left before?
but it was never the right moment, the essential kick delivered,
the fall over that edge, for the knock-through blow...

Each day inside, the spring was wound a little tighter;
another pinch of Semtex added to the heap in my head;
the rope windlassed tighter;
not so easy to walk.

Then coming round on the other side of the bottomless gorge,
it is all over bar the hanging.

At the Dentist

In the dentist
in the magazine
in the quiz

it says

you are on your death bed

do you wish you had spent more time
1   in a phone booth
2   having sex
3   having sex in a phone booth
4   none of the above
5   all the above.

Just then
вдруг – out of the blue, as the saying goes
a crashing MiG-29 takes the roof off the building
exposing the sky.

In the softest ensuing silence, you look down;
a fine film of red dust is settling on the magazine.

My Designer Baby

It has stripes like my cat.
Eyes that light the dark.
No sex: there will be no teenage.

There is a permanent forelock. It does not grow.
The schooling is programmed in.
It loves homework, like cleaning.

It does not feed or eat:
I plug it in at night
in the hallway.

It calls me 'My Lord'.

The Pacific War 1945

Japan would not surrender come what may;
Humans had long forsaken all that's right;
The people of Hiroshima would pay.

Great flights of US bombers flew all day;
Their fire bomb clusters rendered all ash white;
Japan would not surrender come what may.

The soldiers of Japan fought night and day;
Okinawa was held despite their plight;
The people of Hiroshima would pay.

The Kamikaze gave their very clay;
The God Emperor convinced them they were right;
Japan would not surrender come what may.

The Japanese scorned each communiqué;
The Trinity bomb test proved US might;
The people of Hiroshima would pay.

The loaded Superfortress flew all day
To drop its horror at the chosen site;
Japan would not surrender come what may;
The people of Hiroshima would pay.

Brighton Rock Film (2010)

The razors are too new,
the polythene bag on the cafe table out of time,
the Lambrettas too shiny,
the cliff top too high.

We see in one oil painting after another,
the progeny of big bucks filling the screen,
and shiny Brighton as she is in twenty-ten,
not when shaken from the grubby pages of a much-thumbed paperback.

Nowhere is Greene's loose dark chaos menacing,
with a glance like a slice in a cheek
from a treasured jack knife
dealt on the chip-greasy steps.

And even the sea joins the deception;
not spilling from the yellow-edged pages like phlegm,
but spruced up whale blue with happy fame, grinning.

It is not a matter of not suspending disbelief:
it is a matter of conjuring up the read –
and the long ago grey of pain and grief.

The Price of Milk

skeletal cows
summer contorted chequered shapes on green
winter black in coughing sheds
pump out their thirty litres a day

giving up their still damp calves
while Tesco wrings the pennies tight
and we drown cornflakes in white and
swing by the farms without a second glance

First Snow

Leaving Asda
trolley laden
snow falling
Ginny says
be my Sherpa
shoves the trolley over
No
i'm your shirker
she looks fierce like a Gurkha
grab it you gherkin
stop shirkin'
so I steer it
she's gruntled.

We weave
through whitening
a stray flake
sticks
like a feather
on a stray hair
by her lantern face

I pluck it
and eat it.

Magic Monkey Food (*or* When the Cat is Fed)

He waits for his primate to appear
behind the door that opens inwards.
He is too short to pull down the handle
and pull back the door,
only his tail reaches the floor.

He can run at a tree and up it
to trap a bird or squirrel,
but these monkeys have a trick or two
he can't follow.

Monkey appears
chatters
you know what is coming
your mouth waters
you jump up on the side
nothing to see
nothing to smell
this monkey has caught nothing.

Then smell, the most amazing smell.
Riches.
Michelin-starred product of a crazed feline god,
a nostril assault, knocks the breath out of you.
You jump and leap and dance.

You inspect the altar of food on the floor.
Empty.
But your monkey, bends, creaking
mumbo jumbo over the altar
and the delicious entrails are spread before you and you alone.
A feast.

The monkey leaves, their ritual complete.
Suddenly you are alone.
You gobble as fast as you can
before the inevitable
unwelcome reinforcements arrive from behind every bush
beyond the cat flap.

YODEL and the Squirrel

His bushy tail streaming like a comet,
his dash quick and straight,
our scrawny slippery grey creature,
the star of this life then death tale,
makes a break for the always-greener trees
across the sheet of wet tarmac,
with its white dots down the middle that might somewhere
finally say 'Cut Here'.

But, look out, Pikku Orava,
the careering fang-white van,
hell-bent on progress,
has a plump roundabout in its sight,
soon to be conquered with two flicks of the wheel.
See the squirrel's instant peril – with added hot water.

But then
as we crane forward in our plush velvet seats, silent mouths
akimbo,
against all our great expectations,
this scurrying blur is registered somewhere inside the
machine,
and lo and behold, there's a momentary check in the
corporate wheel of fortune,
its oft blind eye, for a split second,
aware.
And hallelujah, our squirrel escapes to cross another day.

On Reflection

Whilst all around the waters shimmer bright,
rippled by the Sirocco's breath of fate,
as I pause to consider what is right,
the mirage fades to sand and won't reflate.
Then I look upon that far shore and see
a speck of hope across the bleak flat land,
a vital pool of life marked by a tree,
the gift of an oasis, by your hand.
Going there to find your welcoming smile –
do I need your acquiescence to drink?
By a careful nod you deem me worthwhile,
and a chain of life is forged link by link.
Then reflecting on our mutual stasis
our gaze holds firm in the deep oasis.

Living in the Styx

look around you and lament with me
for we are in the Styx
in that space that is betwixt
Hades and the generous land and sea

it is hard to raise great ramparts
when underfoot is marsh
when lighting dull but harsh
sucks the strength from our hearts

for we live in Warrington's barren nest
devoid of culture's succour
being taken for a sucker
out of sync with all the rest

of England with its glorious past
nothing has happened here
to boast about or shed a tear
to enter here is to be outcast

little do they know what treasures hide
forgotten like a lost race
forever with a silent face
beneath our feet where we reside

A Rail against Sedition

Our life has military imprecision;
no one left can make a decision;
all our ideas are met with derision;
we're in an impossible position.

This brings us to the brink of a collision
with every Tom and Dick's superposition
leading to concern or suspicion
that we are plotting their demolition.

We must overcome their superstition,
and without the stigma of admission,
lead them straight to the point of cognition,
allowing them the joy of transition.

The danger is immediate ignition,
leading to deep fracture and partition;
a desperate, worrying condition;
and war of bitter endless attrition.

So we must act without inhibition,
reading our enemy's disposition,
to bring the conflict into remission
thus quenching the embers of sedition.

Any ensuing thorough inquisition
will reveal how our essential mission
saved much work for soldier and mortician
and led the way to total contrition.

It's not that we look for recognition;
that was never in our proposition;
it's just the skill of a rhetorician
mimics a true genius magician.

And so, whilst we do lack all ambition
for recompense from any patrician,
we are proud upholders of tradition
and thereby hope to escape perdition.

Message in a Bottle

There are times, and this is one,
when a scribbled 'HELP' hastily rolled then pressed down the
neck of a to-be-tightly-corked bottle
is the only rational action of a sane man.

Peer through the hard glass, see the note sitting poised
like a lizard on a branch, its single word in blazing 1950s
neon.
Encapsulated, it defies all but time.

Once lobbed bobbing onto the conveying ocean and watched
out of sight
there is nothing to do but sit under a palm tree
to await the eager Super Puma helicopter
even now refuelling in Syracuse.

The short investigation carried out on arrival reveals;
'Death by coconut, sometime in the early 21st century'.
The chalky bones, gathered in her holdall, feel light to the
smiling pilot.

New Town Anarchist

PART I

i went to the shops
to buy me some bread
but dhillon told me
the baker is dead

i walked to croft
to steel me a car
but my shoes fell apart
i didnt get far

i wish i were blond
the girls go for that
but i can fool them
i wear a big hat

they soon fall for me
with my mystery head
and when i get home
i wear it in bed

then afterwards
i do a reveal
and they slam the door
i do a cartwheel

my dog ate my cat
the boa ate him
i ate the boa
except for the skin

so i live alone
and bake my own bread
now the dog and cat
and boa are dead

PART II

i cut down a tree
to burn me some wood
cos my house is cold
being made of mud

i went to protest
against the fracking
but the mad crusties
soon sent me packing

i ate their baked beans
and fell over the tent
leaving them hungry
and their home all bent

when the police turned up
waving their truncheons
i sneaked in their van
and ate their luncheons

the coppers got mad
and placed all the blame
on the bearded leader
garys his name

he took against me
had me evicted
ironic is that
law unrestricted

so i need a cause
to get out of bed
now saving us all
is a path i cant tread

birchwood is empty
no place for a god
I think I'll go south
but stay on my tod

I'll go to the sea
and the sun will shine
I'll pack in this lot
and have a good time

Man Apart

i am not very good with women's names

i see them sitting across the road in cafe windows
staring at their nails

the light is unkind to them
harsh

they have been plucked from the soft rainforest
and placed on a shelf for misunderstanding
lit for selling

their feet squeezed into agony have forgotten the moss
on rocks wriggling with toes giggling
that flat freedom to follow the contours of the mind

their life, an upward struggle to gain a few inches in height, as
the water rises
and too few arms, for their burdens

i am never very good with women's names

my life is easy, the privilege
it all falls in my lap

doors open, smiling, my salary is raised
with a nod, any wish granted

at my height I can see over walls
yet I walk alone, eat alone, and sleep alone

no, I am not very good with women's names
each is like a depth charge to me

Sunshine

Walking side by side, the words spill easy
across the afternoon. There's so little
air in the conversation that my watch
spins around unseen. Then, finding a warm
spot where the light reaches far to a view,
we pause and turn to face one another
for the first time, dancing like butterflies
in welcome of a new dawn, knowing we
have the whole day to play. The hours vanish
down a sink hole of pleasure, each word sipped
from the rare elixir that is youth, each
memory a treasured fragment of life
to be mulled over when we are apart
in separate lives in the same world close by.

Cyborg

Aldous Huxley had it right, you know – for now begins the year of Our Ford one-seven-six.
Of course, it would have been twenty thirty-nine in the year of our old Lord.

These hands you see before you are not quite what you think; suitably pink and clean, yes, but the skin is plastic, and soft as Fairy Liquid gel.

I have had it replaced all over, and the under-wrinkles zapped.
Oh, and by the way, that upgrade to my heart pump has improved my tennis.

Why are my eyes so blue? – aren't they just? There's no point on skimping on the lapis lazuli.
And my ear implants can pick out your dulcet tones from this vast care-home crowd at thirty paces.

Best of all, my tongue of the softest suede can persuade, and will assuage, as never before,
backed as it is by my hairy memory scull-cap – well, the newly upgraded get all the best lines.

It is fun shopping for exoskeletons – we must change it every solar-year like the mutant spider-crabs we are – I like that shiny new black number with the titanium bands and the tight rubber grommets – the straps worn like the Blondie I think I remember as a kid in Blackpool back when.

Humming away to itself, my stainless steel digestion minds its own business.
Needs no stirring or emptying like the cauldrons and hoppers of old.

No matter my head is quite empty and lightly air-conditioned
against damp and rot in the sinuses;
being light-headed is *par for the course* these days, to use a
lost metaphor from those distant days of unbridled
photosynthesis, grass, and air open to the sky.

But best of all we are always happy happy – the tablet sees
to that. Replenished while we sleep – down that little extra
hatch we never had before, more of a window on our missing
soul, than a door.

The Legacy of 'The Snail'

We stand before the altar of Matisse,
a bold square collage patchwork called 'The Snail',
eleven colours coiled in a lattice,
at ten thousand inches square, vast in scale.
His first pictures, bold and brightly painted,
have their brave lines drawn from a future time,
with a purity that's yet untainted,
ennobling colour like the perfect rhyme.
He pushed a new ultra-vision of life,
reflecting the brave century he was in;
whether working with a brush or a knife,
he strove to raise his work above the din.
Yet in deep old age, with his skilled hands spoiled,
he was left directing, as others toiled.

The Day Before

Although you must be wondering,
ask not about the dawn or the evening,
for it was the day broad as daylight,
the sun high and the hours ranged full,
when we strolled on that expanse
hitherto known only as a place to be alone.

Although you must be curious,
ask not about the fish or the oystercatchers,
for they were intent on their own purpose,
leaving us the space to be together –
lapping the light and softly approaching
the doffing water that is without end.

Although you have your reasons,
ask not about the fox or the rabbit,
for they played chase in the sharp grass
and let us pass heard but unseen –
the baking warmth from the sand hillocks
pressing us to move on into the cloaking pines.

Although you may feel some concern,
ask not of that child or squirrel,
for they ran free and only wondered at us,
letting us traverse their domain –
the rich perfume of the pines
leading the assault of the acid needles.

Although you must be about to burst,
ask not when the log tide of talk ended,
for the hours were free as air and fatly
remained full of life and breath –
and memory's roving eye allows the pleasure
to play again like a bird taking flight over water.

Beloved
(After 'When You are Old' by W B Yeats)

How many loved your moments of glad grace,
And loved your beauty with love false or true,
But one man loved the pilgrim soul in you,
And loved the sorrows of your changing face;

This once in life I struck a deep rich vein,
that filled a crowd of days with rain or sun.
Time spent with you in mind is life indeed,
a fullness gained from drinking water cool,
a deep oasis after mirage seen,
that mirage having all but left no trace.
To hear as you performed your deep-felt work,
all those created life-lines freely shared,
delivered with aplomb and lively pace;
how many loved your moments of glad grace.

The long-drawn dawn of childhood held you firm,
with pomp and circumstance that English way,
then as your life-road forked you found your course;
convention beat the bed of closest warmth.
You strived and gave so much of mother love,
the world took all and then did misconstrue,
and yet the race was on to be hard won,
without an overt seeking or display,
from those who did admire and follow you,
and loved your beauty with love false or true.

Your years of toil and caring were behind,
that journey through a world of twisting light,
that laid a sway of memory locked in place,
the time well spent in forging your strong core.
But once the feathered nest was rightly flown,
you thought that all who saw you looked right through,
though here and there a spark remained aglow,
each day became a place of stillborn hope,
while cloaked your angel-wings were hidden too,
but one man loved the pilgrim soul in you.

He gained his place by gentle hours of grace,
to learn and feel the outside and the in,
to share in offered trust and find a world
that he did not believe could all be his:
to make time, as an athlete training hard,
to gain the prize of winning, soul and race,
to acknowledge each day lived in with you,
to seek and enjoy your soft tender ways.
He has found life afresh in this fond place,
and loved the sorrows of your changing face.

The Silver Pocket Watch

Inside, the mercurial-gold mechanism
sits out the decades silent as a thought,
awaiting an awakening, the twisting of the key
that will return life's spark to its iron sprung heart.

Then, pocketed close by my happy heart,
it will repeat away my time. Its tick limping
like my rheumy silver muzzled dog, always behind,
heavy tail wagging, ambition replete.

So many times viewed, with a lost uncle's soft chuckle,
or darkened brow of alarm at the train leaving town,
and kept chained, to be wound slow, deep in thought:
it alone has marked the long deep of the attic days.

So let it speak: Inside my case a silver 'e';
King George then young and sane.
Open my bull's eye glass, find the pierced balance cock,
four square pillars, the verge and fusee.

Returning Child

Just when you have your family tree just so,
a knock at the door.
Standing there, with a question mark and a smile,
is an unknown familiar like a long-lost raincoat
from the back of your cupboard,
asking to come inside.

There was this other life.
Your wife puts on the kettle in the kitchen.
His name is like any other,
but his origin is down a time tunnel
in the stars.
A reeling bird circles the house,
announcing.

There is this other life.
I imagine he's heavy,
he is certainly bulky.
Thinking I cannot brush him under the mat,
I introduce him to Mary,
in exchange for the tea she brings us,
as my son.

Stillborn

That poem you did not write – the idea flowing clear like
spring water from a holy well –
is a child you never had:

A gap – not as in teeth – but as in a chasm separating
continents in the grip of a necrotic war.
That life, that influence, of its own space, beating out
uniqueness like Pauli,
dissipated to a future wrapped in the past –
safe and disarmed, blank and toothless, tucked away
inside itself, and forever.

And then there is the forgetting – like that space between two
pages of a closed book.
How can you remember what has never been?
Did you give her a chance to breathe?
All it takes is a bit of inflation – we run almost on automatic.
You would not have needed to help – she would help herself:
Gushing forth, the spring water cold as a razor-eye, she
would dissect in you a fresh future.
Reeling, you would fly across the landscape anew.

Cycle Path

Walking along the pavement, there is a white line painted down the middle.
But which side of the line is the footpath and which side is the cycle path?
I do not know - there is no way to tell - I want to run away.
I proceed with caution - looking behind me rather too often.

But coming towards me now is a large cyclist, travelling fast.
Has he seen me? I think not. His head is down.
Now, is he on the cycle path, or is he a psychopath?
I am wondering this as his silhouette grows ever larger.

What is this painted on the pavement? Two symbols with two wheels.
They are bikes. So that is the cycle path. I am on the footpath. Good.
But wait. The cyclist, he is on the footpath too.
So he is a psychopath.

I jump onto the cycle path just in time
avoiding the psychopath as he flashes past,
bent on swallowing up the miles or killing someone or both.
But what shall I do now? Where is it safe to walk?

I proceed down the white line, making myself very thin,
but very obvious, by puffing up my chest and walking with stiff legs,
then any passing cyclists or psychopaths will hopefully just sail on by,
and I will make it home to my seventh birthday party in one piece, after all.

Gandalf and the Traffic Warden

It is at times like this -
the day a wet Bank Holiday Monday -
when I remember

that mind-popping prequel,
set in our Northern Town,
where oft we roam like theropods.

Being able, and able to be anywhere,
in the way of multiverses,
one day he was here.

He left his craft against the kerb,
going in search of sustenance,
and to discern his whereabouts.

Yet Gandalf knew not
what significance
had been attached long ago in smoky rooms

to the metal sign that stood,
text plain and spelling good,
with times clear writ.

It took him seventy minutes to get his lunch and bearings,
to know that leaving was wise.
He returned to his craft.

A flat capped Warden was in attendance.
The officer did not scratch his head
at the sleek shape, instead

he was writing in his book of slips.
He did not look up.
He tore off the slip.

Gandalf stepped into his craft.
The paper was silently adhered.
The craft rose and vanished.

The Warden had turned away.
He was recording a number in his book.
The thin rain continued.

Nanobot Hero Soup

Injected and swimming
in your blood like commandoes
dropped into France
they seek and find the enemy bacteria

that will otherwise kill you.
Latching on, they swarm, cluster, organise,
find the flagellum for I D, "Tango",
commence drilling and dive in.

Selflessly, taking chemical casualties,
they throttle the devil from within and,
laying a tiny charge that would blow the foot off a flea,
dismember its nucleus.

This bacterium and millions more
reduced to stagnant jelly,
the nanobots make their escape
back into the hammering blood.

Their job done, as one they head for your eye
for extraction, R&R, and refuelling,
before the next needle.
You, the patient, gratefully recover.

Stirrings

Looking from the back window across the gardens,
the Fiddler's Ferry chimney stands like Nelson's column.
Nelson is absent, having gone for a short walk,
and is now causing consternation on the pavement below.

There is something egotistical about that space above the chimney,
claimed once by the all-obscuring smoke in its rush to find
freedom of expression.

We hope a volunteer will step forward, stand still and be noticed,
to have heroism heaped upon them like pitch-forked manure,
before sinking paginated into libraried history,
fit for the statue-maker's eye and the expenditure of public money.

And now the smoke is finally gone forever from that place,
we are going to put a woman up there.
She will stand in full view, unblinking,
her stone hair rigid like her stone heart,
her arms captured and fixed in that flailing motion
designed to keep the pigeons flying on by.

She will balance her way into our futures,
remote and unfocused,
her presence felt like a speck of grit in our eye,
and leave us fearing at every juncture which way to turn,
being Cleopatra, Boudicca and Thatcher all rolled into one.

Where

I imagine running with you on golden sand
Pressed between toes
Laughing to the laughing blue water
To swim free
To run and taste the wind
To lie in the dusty warmth

To see green, hear gentle summer sounds
On days so long that they wrap around
And fingers on clock time stick in the afternoon

To gently tease away the edges of the mind
Leaving a flood of calm

Taking in real life on an island

Seventeen

I can feel in your presence the significance of the moment
You are seventeen and engaged
You read a childcare book
Thinking of your man

His ring, a recent addition to your pale finger,
Stirs admiration from your merry girl friends
Its gold band and white glint promise a hard future
Cold as the unknown, an unfolding of life

Your young body is pale, pure and soft as dawn light
But warm
Your eyes have in them the flecks of love
Hope smoulders quietly in your breast

An edge has been reached
And your mother? Oh she doesn't mind
For now you are the future,
                              the warmth,
You are ready to carry the burdens of life
Accept the brutality of truth, as any mother does

Go in peace...

No Shirt

Peeling off my anorak
underneath is skin

blistered and blotched
numbers tattooed in ranks

caved chest
breathing a little

human being
being concentrated here

concentration here
on skin

anorak back on
going, going on

Anne

My world of warmth
Carrying my children
Feeding my world

Feeding my love
Shielding the dark
Filling the void

Holding my life
Stretching my being
My half life

Soft tethered to you
Yielding my youth
Creating new life

Talking to Elaine

You are brimming full – to be drained only once.
Suffering has bled you – your substance like dried grass.

As you sit and caress the air with gentle tones
Your age shimmers before you before vanishing.

Now, you are a child again,
And your eyes pool upwards into your mother's.

As the wrinkles fall from your face,
With relaxation, you find grace.

Of that Told by Primo Levi

Let me say: Do not turn away
Do not forget
Do not question

For truth screams out
Never to be hidden by silence
Never to be questioned

The unbidden pain
Driven by unfathomable men
So recent
Soiling our prayers

Now we know
Our tears burn
And tiny screams reach us from the void
To smash us – let them guide us

Fracture those minds closed
Feed them with oozing honey
Return feeling
Teach, teach...

Outside Spacetime

Let me out – freedom spirits august reason
Sending each thought with passion

Think of here as bent from time
The objects fickle as young love

Think as soul forever bent away from time
To stand spired through reality forever

Think of body as ruled by rules
Subject to a cliff top fall

Think of love – love beyond reason
As lasting outside the universal all

Meeting souls meld in fever
Allow the dot forever to fuse

As death removes from clock world
This moment – it can never close

Sleeping Child

This day is done for you
And your new toy is forgotten on the floor
Your future stretches and yawns to swallow you
- You cannot take me with you
- You will not be yourself forever
Needs are filled by the moment
Pass on my secrets
As the chain of life passes to you

Needs Must

I took my love for you and drowned it like a kitten
but I will still talk to you now and then.
As the body rots inside, only the soft fur is left.
But I remember that look from those eyes;
the irretrievable flicker of life is remembered
but lost in the tight mouth and eyes of death.

Can we expect civility when cymbals crash in mind?
Why split open the wound sewn so tight?
When might a relaxed air rest between us?
How long can the anguish crush each move?
When are the embers too cold to be rekindled?

Who can resurrect my pretty soft drowned kitten love?

Death at My Birth Averted

had i been allowed to die i
would have been there,
an extra at heaven's party,
pure, perhaps a little slow on the uptake,
but warm and cosy with you all.

but i lived by decanted blood and 60s tricks,
and becoming divided by trivia
am a lost dead soul among the living now,
committing crime in suburban banal precincts
and a blackness covers me.

so does fire await me on that
dawn when satisfying
the final
call

Loose End

I can't even urinate with enthusiasm these days.

The black pools around my eyes haunt me in the mirror.

I once was blond and shone like steel,
but now I am dulled with the wooden drudgery born of serfdom.

I thought I could break free,
beat a system set up to pervert life,
but now I know that the grip round my throat will tighten with time
and, that if I cut off the hands that strangle me,
I will only fall sooner into the abyss.

Seeking refuge in the banal will only prolong my existence
and hardly appease the many hungry wolves already
gathering at my funeral.

Remember, small recompense needs to be paid only to those
directly involved in my life,
as the majority have given nothing.

Letting myself slip from here might be a relief,
only who is to say the cradle will be rocked more gently in the next world?

Sonnet 14

Shall I compare thee to Cameron Diaz
Thou art somewhat shorter and more hairy
But roughly the same shape about the ears
And your broad smile is equally leery
Sometimes your coiffure is not quite so slick
And oft reminds one of a rodent's nest
But you have your people to fix it quick
A lick and a shake and you look your best
While she's a pin-up on many a wall
You feature mostly on coin of the realm
And on stamps too – where you are very small
But size is not all, you are at the helm –
When there's a crisis and terrible fears
We all look to you – not Cameron Diaz

I

I am
I am free
I am free as
I am free as a
I am free as a bird

I am free as a bird's eye
I am free as a bird's eye fish
I am free as a bird's eye fish finger
I am free as a bird's eye fish finger frozen
I am free as a bird's eye fish finger frozen in

I am free as a bird's eye fish finger frozen in permafrost

Princess

Your concentrated radiance filled the hall,
dimming the thousands present to dusk.

Slippery light played tricks with your features,
your eyes shining,
your long, long hair invoking the poetry of perfection
with a blondness pure as molten orgiastic love.

The poet springs to life, injected with a thousand needles
and lives with you
    breathes with you
        possesses your being

and sensing the formal measure of the moment, captures
beauty in the eye, the heart, the souls

and all transgression is possible
    all transfiguration is possible.

Thus reality performs for the poet.

The Sea

Wooden splint – whales squint
Eyeful tower
Fill the sewer
Rendered cheese
Pleased with these
By Blackpool Tower

Waved at the spray
Which went away – left the beach
Sling, sling mud
Travel by tub
Steer with wood
Strand in Wales

Lash and burn – lost jelly
Jetty smelly boat, fish daily
Oiled welly
Fish quick silver
Rotten diver stuck – no luck

Human mounting waves
White chested, crested
Tooth and sail
Slops in the pale at dawn
Ping goes the prawn
And this swell sucks

Wash the seal and wish
Now the sole is in the dish
Forget the tail
The head is lost
Pardon any sharkened girl
For losing herself in the swirl

Flames will burn the sky to white
And black will sabotage the night
Deep down the prowling angels
Swimming in the dungeon ocean
Will keep the planet's secret
When we are gone

Woman

That you are
there to envelope
to hold dear
to share
is enough

That you are there
to hold me
grow me
mould me
is more

That you are there to
provide light
still pain
warm me
is life

That you are there to form
my life
my soul
my purpose
is divine

Woman – cradle me with your love

Another Day

hanging on in there and casually asking for the world
to tip a little more into the light
the park – it is warm out there at lunchtime
and not so lonely when a tall and elegant girl walks too
and chats away half an hour in the sun and sudden breeze
and no fooling, this is a request that cannot be left longer –
it has to happen now
so I will push a little and not take a no for an answer because
we live so few warm days on this planet
by arrangement with our genes and so much else cooking in
the cells

and this tall conditioned dark girl has so much left to do
and there is suffering in her future that cannot be taken and
swallowed
even by a lover who wishes to take the pain and swallow
away all the future
so the asking and basking in the warm sun in the park
will not happen I am guessing because there is always a
reason why
the end is the same and a provoking nature has no way of
redoubling its effort
it is a spent thing
so I will try and touch a moment in the sun
and as previously it is expected that I would walk
alone

i will have to explain this in words of one syllable
because it is so simple
the days they pass, have past, will pass, if they are there

so little is happening
so little is working

when will it occur and how?

It's Easy

Welcome, sundry Humans, to spaceship 'Enlightenment'.
Your journey will take approximately two of your Earth minutes.
Please sit and relax a moment.

Now, look out forwards through the window at the space station centre point marker.
Close your eyes.
Imagine the length of the distance you have just seen, as you have been taught.
Now shrink yourself inside your head until you are a black dot.
Feel that you are weightless, tiny, out of space and time.

Now remember the distance to the marker and think of each one of your ten fingers.
Increase the distance in your head by ten times.
Hold it.

Think of your ten fingers and increase it again.
Hold this distance – the baseline of about ten kilometres is achieved.
Imagine and increase again by ten.
Now imagine your line of ten in a cube of one thousand – ten by ten by ten.
Pull them in your mind and string them out row after row.
See the thousand and multiply your distance by this factor.
Hold the distance.

Think of the thousand dots in a cube again, line them up and multiply the distance again.
See the length of the line.
The distance you can see is the distance from your Sun to the Earth.

See the thousand and extend the line.
See 500 and extend the line. Add ten more.
Good.
Hold it.
Now take your mind point and 'step' across to the other end.
Hold it.

Feel that you are complete.
Hold it.
If anyone is lost at the moment, please hold up your hand.
Good.

Now you are ready – let go of the line from your head – feel the snap.
Good – open your eyes.

We have arrived in your solar system, your shuttle craft will be leaving shortly for Earth.
Please check your calendar has adjusted correctly: Today is 27th July 2117.
Please take all your belongings with you as you leave the spacecraft.
Virgin Hops thanks you for your custom.
We look forward to seeing you again soon.

Justine

Soft warm slip of flame
The melted pauses of your smile
Carry me to your eyes of jet

Young untamed careless careful jewel
Filled with expression
Shaped to your lover's need

Falling away to new worlds
Spirit twisting untethered
Where will you find rest?

Find a rock of reason
Allow a nest, a home
Welcome the living there

She Beyond Memory

it was those eyes
in that setting
walking that way
those colours
so slender so free
that life that leg
those agile looks
and then the nearness
radiance
flickers of meaning
gentle innocence
playful eyes
happiness
relaxing
calming
being
those eyes
deep and slender
ready with love
shining with the day
radiating You
that hair
pure, long
graced with soft light
bouncing gentleness
curtaining your soul
challenging the sun

and your knight bows
kneeling beside the poet
and the world stops turning
truth and beauty meld here
fire and life
and life and fire mingling
we that are worthy salute you, our divine

The Lonesome Log

Seaweed, seagull on the rock
Rest your elbow on the shock
Dive in the brash and wag about
Until the hashish wallows out

Set the eyes as wide apart
As willow axes for the dart
Understand the edge of foes
Before the brittle onyx grows

Swallow down the quicksome brine
Bellow forth a second time
Hope that when the eye is clear
The pupil will have twisted near

Goggle and fuggle round nearby
Because the fetid never try
Push the flattened board away
And goad the hive bees 'til they stay

Mentioning the other side
Is likely not to tan the pride
Of lions green, sprats debonair
With mermen rid of golded hair

Now fancy listening to a grape
When we are grasping in the nape
With warm air and graces often loose
– I have forgone the hanging noose

Please reckon up the language pale
Steeling along the pardonable rail
To guard the winsome rind about
And teach some poetry to this lout

Night Verses

Let me record here and now that the blackness will soon fade as the world has done: even the lone wolf has gone.

I looked though the pamphlet and there was no poetry.

Six years is a life.

In the room where a son was born the black will soon fade. Day named Saturday – a token to the space – will continue the thoughts.

Drop the pretences. We all know that bags of wind and flesh perish.
Be an uplifting bag of wind and flesh. This is history in the making.

We have not come far. But around and about lie the rest.

Paris, London, will not burn this time round, dear 21st Century of care.
Peace be with the rusty war mongers. Yet a few burn still in the dark night.

Are you threatened with eternal damnation? We've set that aside now as a curiosity.
We gaze heavenwards and count. Lonely isn't it?

Face facts, says nobody: if the future could come here, it would be here now.
Our dust is all there is…

Desolation

That tick again
That drip
That drip again

There are no walls
The prison is time
The prison is a valley without you
The desert prison
The desert

The waiting
The waiting in silence
The soft dust
The soft rolling dust
The rolling hours
The hours

The hunger
The waiting
The cold desert
The desert prison
The prison without you
The prison without walls
The prison

That drip again
That drip
That tick again

Washing Incompetence is Nothing to Boast About

There are no boxers left in my drawer, again.
Ranting, in a long gown, I go in search.
They are all still in the washer, lying wet and dark.
I return to my sock drawer swearing.

Then, as I slip on y-fronts,
which I never wear,
I remember with a start
dear King John
losing all his clothes in the Wash:
he has never lived it down –
incompetence has clung leech-like through eight centuries.

Sighing, I decide to say nothing more, and avoid peaches.

Around and About

we have reached out now into a new stabbing twenty-first century
and the guns are silent
we have no need of guns
the world is so small we have wrap-around and laugh-around, sharing the same jokes

each cluster of family people has a base and reason enough to live on
with no further use for guns
talking is the order of the days and nights
the world is tiny and voices travel all around so all hear and feel included

so what is this? A voice from the wilderness backed by gunpowder and mean little eyes
and such righteous might, carrying his guns
from across a little way and setting stall
the world is yet shrinking and we will hear the screams now even in this house with children

say excuse me and lock your arm on his and ask why the guns
we are grown now
we have no use for guns
and in the small corner where he resides he sits low, yet I can see his beady eyes from here

and his people are frightened by the igniting powder and planes and dark eyed men unseen
who are pressed to find guns
who are driven to take up guns
and the small world where they are laid broken at their feet
and they cry but carry on

the conflagration in this small world flashes round on itself
and unleashes harm
the guns speak
no good comes from this
we are pulled back to feast on might as the beady eyes take
their will with might

yet here and there we will not stomach this and will not agree
to follow the might
we have no use for guns
no good comes from destruction
in the new world we talk and laugh with all the same people
around us

500 Words on the Inside of a Ping Pong Ball

This is a space not often contemplated
but moved violently at our whim and to the rules of flight.
As I look, I can imagine the space in there where organic molecules fly,
looking for a way out from a serious continuity.

Is it dark inside? During the day I think not.
There is a smooth light, whitened, dull as toothache.
It hovers.
At night there is a black stone within, powder soft.
It listens.

Travel round with me now on the inside, that eggshell curve
so unnatural to a bird – nothing points the way.
Tap and try to escape, from our holy white blankness,
into the roaring, jagged, fierceness of fractal space.

We are dimensionless in here
and bound as if by a forgotten treaty.
We are glum
and do not even nod to each other across the space within.

Wait.
There is a ridge, an equator.
We are of two halves,
sealed like lips of the grim.

This line, this circle of orientation, holds promise and fuels our fantasies
of outside glamorous disasters,
of luck, and of an end to anything.
We that are without end, salute you that are without.

This is harder than I thought.
There is a tiny space to describe.
It dwarfs an ant – an ant being its opposite;
all tiny edges, limbs, decisions, and work to carry a future.

The inside of the ball lacks a voice, like an extinct race.
The inside surface would offer resistance but cannot be
accessed, just out of sight.
The inside is there now, but for all time?
No, it can and will be violated.

A stamping foot crushes a demon's smile into the roundness.
A sharp probe penetrates into the space like a death seen
from the inside.
The atmosphere of the ball so punctured becomes mingled
with our crowded air.
Shouts and alarms reach the interior unbridled.

There is a new dawn with no separation.
This unnatural object has a manufactured odour.
An aromatic pong, acrid and alarming,
emanates from within a punctured ball.

There has been no escape since its capture
at the very moment of moulding
in that lightest of factories
in some unimagined distant land.

The world over, there are these little spaces, like in our
hearts; so quiet.
Lying in drawers, out on tables, or somewhere and out of
sight.

They are waiting to be taken and bounced around at our whim.
We need not be careful, there are plenty to go round: we are in control.

In the course of time, the inside smoothness might give way to a coarse hairiness.
This would be so inappropriate.
It would make the ball heavier, darker, unreasonable, prone to violence, not to be trusted.
It will not happen.

There are no corners.
There is nowhere to hide.
I am running out of ideas and, looking in for inspiration, I find a small blank space behind my eyes.
I blink and we are done.

Printed in Great Britain
by Amazon